# PoMo Poverty

### Finding Abundance in the 21st Century

## Tom Spence

*Tom Spence*

Copyright

©2011 by Tom Spence.

All rights reserved.

## PoMo Poverty

Tom Spence

God told them, *I've never quit loving you
and never will.*
  *Expect love, love, and more love!*


Jeremiah 31:3 (*The Message*)

## Poverty or Paradox

In early 1981, I was hiking into the Philippine jungle with my platoon behind me. I was the third platoon back on the company march along a very narrow trail in which it was difficult for two Marines to walk abreast of each other. We were in the boonies for sure.

After a couple hours of walking, the trail opened up.

To our left was a fair sized house made out of C-Ration cardboard. What ingenuity! What genius. What poverty. A family was living in a house made out of discarded cardboard.

Don't get me wrong, C-Rat cardboard is the best in the world for waterproofing. It has a fair insulation value. It is sturdy.

How do I know this?

In many a cold and wet moment, a piece of C-Rat cardboard was just the insulation from the cold or wet ground that I needed to get a couple hours of sleep.

These people had built an entire house out of the stuff, to include what seemed to be a garage, at least there was a garage door sized opening that faced the trail which brought us past this unique site. But there was no car in the garage, not even a Jeepney or a bicycle.

Instead, there was a beautiful pool table around which were gathered some young men who seemed to be enjoying themselves and nearly oblivious to our passing.

What a contrast. What a dichotomy. What a paradox. We were witness to luxury within poverty.

Or was this poverty?

The shelter was adequate.

The people were happy.

The jungle was full of food.

It obviously took some sort of income to purchase the table and transport it to this site.

Was this poverty?

What is poverty?

This is 2011, so instead of thumbing through my Webster's, I found a most comprehensive definition at Dictionary.com. It follows.

**pov·er·ty**  [pov-er-tee]

noun

1.  the state or condition of having little or no money, goods, or means of support; condition of being poor. Synonyms: privation, neediness, destitution, indigence, pauperism, penury. Antonyms: riches, wealth, plenty.

2.  deficiency of necessary or desirable ingredients, qualities, etc.: poverty of the soil. Synonyms: thinness, poorness, insufficiency.

3.  scantiness; insufficiency: Their efforts to stamp out disease were hampered by a

poverty of medical supplies. Synonyms: meagerness, inadequacy, sparseness, shortage, paucity, dearth. Antonyms: abundance, surfeit, sufficiency, bounty, glut.

The United States Census Bureau, using a plethora of information and formulae, has defined 48 thresholds of poverty. The income range for poverty in America is roughly between eleven thousand dollars for an individual to forty-two thousand dollars for a very large family.

Wikipedia contributed the following to the definition.

**Poverty** is the state of one who lacks a certain amount of material possessions or money. Absolute poverty or **destitution** refers to being unable to afford basic human needs, which commonly includes clean and fresh water, nutrition, health care, education, clothing and shelter.

About 1.7 billion people are estimated to live in absolute poverty today. Relative poverty refers to lacking a usual or socially acceptable level of resources or income as compared with others within a society or country.

And even in 2011, we cannot exclude Mr. Webster entirely in defining **poverty**.

1   a: the state of one who lacks a usual or socially acceptable amount of money or material possessions b: renunciation as a member of a religious order of the right as an individual to own property

2: scarcity, dearth

3   a: debility due to malnutrition b: lack of fertility

A somewhat synthesized definition proved by the search engine Google is:

pov•er•ty

noun   /'pävərtē/

1.      The state of being extremely poor

> *- thousands of families are living in abject poverty*

2.      The state of being inferior in quality or insufficient in amount

> *- the poverty of her imagination*

3.      The renunciation of the right to individual ownership of property as part of a religious vow


So did this Philippine family live in poverty?

By income standards to which I have grown accustomed, yes.  They were outright poor.

By possessing the means to meet their needs, no.  These people had an abundance.

This was a paradox of poverty.  There was abundance without wealth as we define wealth these days.  There appeared to be happiness and contentment in this snapshot view.

There was no further explanation or exploration of this circumstance. When you are a Marine on the move, you make your observations quickly. Assessments may come over time.

We don't see homeless people in the part of the United States where I live. Somehow, some way, they find shelter.

We don't see C-Rat houses here either.

Perhaps homelessness is big in the big cities, but most of the population of this nation does not live in the big cities. They live near cities so as to have access to what metropolitan areas have to offer, but for the most part, they live semi-rural areas. Even many who once lived in the suburbs have sought something a little more rural.

Homelessness is not an issue in most of America, but surely poverty is.

*Tom Spence*

We live in what many consider a post modern world.  So what does post modern poverty look like?

That will be the first part of this essay.

The second will be to answer the question, "What can we do about it?"

## Money

We have to start with money, right?

Most poverty definitions are about not having enough money to meet basic needs, make ends meet, or to live as comparatively well as the social and economic norm of the country in which poverty is defined.

So let's look at poverty from a monetary perspective. What is the poverty threshold in this country from a monetary viewpoint?

The answer is not a dollar value but an item for which so many will forgo paying the water bill to maintain.

What?

The cell phone. Actually, the cell phone is so 20th century. Smart phone or personal communication device would surely be closer to what folks can't be without today.

I meet with people weekly who are about to have their water turned off in the summer or gas turned off in the winter, who have the top of the line smart phones and usually several hundred dollars worth of past due phone bills to go with the devices.

These are folks in and out of work, not top level executives who need to stay on top of calls, messages, emails, and web applications. The future of the business is not hanging in the balance. The water bill is hanging in the balance. It needs to be paid more than these folks need the immediate gratification of being able to post an online note that says, "Smoked my last. No, I'm not quitting, I'll just bum until the kid's welfare checks come in. LOL."

In another month their phone service will be cut off because they will be a thousand dollars in the hole to the provider, but the water will get cut off before they give up their phones. It will be a little harder to add "LOL" to the end of that day.

When some of these people do get jobs, they lose them because they are on their smart phone all the time when they should be flipping burgers or moving pipe.

Computers, cell phones, smart phones, and even smarter phones are not evil. They are exceptional tools in the right hands. There was a time that I needed to be connected that well to lead the people and manage the programs entrusted to me. Today, a cell phone with a simple keyboard does just fine.

For most of the people facing termination of utility services, eviction, or smart phone disconnection; spending money on these devices and the package of services is like me owning a backhoe and front end loader. On occasion, I turn over some dirt to plant some bulbs or maybe even till the soil in my small tomato patch. A shovel works just fine. I don't need a hundred or thousand fold the dirt moving capability.

So I don't own one. My bulbs come up just fine each spring.

So my starting point in defining fiscal poverty is the cell phone. It is among the leading indicators of poverty in America.

Hold your smart phone horses! If I have a cell phone, does that mean I live in poverty?

Answer that for yourself. Are you paying all of your bills, giving to your church and charities, and meeting the essential needs of your family? If not, then the answer should be that you are in smart phone poverty.

~

Credit cards and pay day loans are hard to hide. They scream poverty. They scream never-ending debt. They shout, "I shot myself in the foot and I am reloading."

I use credit cards almost every day. They are convenient, offer some protection, and many even offer rewards. So long as I spend only what I have budgeted, I am the master of my credit cards.

People who see credit cards as an open ended answer to unanswered prayer have not been praying to the one true God. Someone else has answered their prayers—petitions to be enslaved in debt are the only answers headed their way.

Payday loan companies give credit cards a run for their poverty money. I have worked a budget with families that had as many as 3 payday loans.

One family of 3 received the equivalent of forty thousand dollars a year in government subsidies yet couldn't keep the water on. By any measure, they should have been living better than the average family in these parts, but every month watched their income (provided courtesy of the taxpayers) evaporate with three short term loan payments. On top of that, they were angry that they couldn't get another loan.

*Tom Spence*

Let's add credit and debt to our definition of post modern poverty.

~

If you need to know for sure that someone is living in poverty in the second decade of this new millennia, check out their furniture. Is it new looking? Is there a big flat screen television in the house with no electricity? It is obviously more than they can afford?

It may be somewhere on the credit card balance, or it more likely came from a furniture rental company.

My office has a window with good visibility over a two hundred yard stretch of the main road in the center of my small town. Several times each day, I see trucks from these two area rental companies going in and out of the housing areas. I have worked with families that have hundreds of dollars in furniture rental fees each month and are about to be evicted from their home because they didn't pay their rent.

Only when I sat down and did a line item budget did they eventually see that their rental furniture depleted their monthly income by almost as much as the rent payment on their home. This is western Oklahoma. For $50 to $100 you can outfit a living room with decent furniture. Key words: yard sale and auction.

Marines make a seat out of their folding entrenching tools. College kids are living large with a couple of cinder blocks and a few boards.

Does that mean that there is never an occasion to rent anything but a home?

No. The family struggling to make ends meet is going to rent that trombone for a few months to see if their son sticks with it or goes back to playing guitar zero in front of the television that mom found for $15 at a yard sale.

If the boy and horn are playing the blues and the neighborhood dogs are not in revolt, then it might be time to find a way to purchase the instrument. If he is already talking about taking advanced calculus instead of band next semester, renting was the way to go.

The poverty of renting is that it makes things that you can't afford appear momentarily affordable. In the process you give up things you needed but now can't afford.

~

The most important indicator of hope is the tithe.

A family that struggles, but continues to tithe will not struggle for long. Trusting God to make 90% go farther than 100% is a sign that individuals and families are sick of financial poverty.

They spent their lives going to churches saying give me, give me, give me.

When they catch a break and get a raise, promotion, or even a better job; they seldom remember to offer the first fruits of that income to God. They don't trust God.

Usually, a few months later, these families are back at church needing something again.

Only when people trust God in the midst of their poverty, do we see hope emerge.

I have been through this struggle. Only when I committed to give 10% of my income, off the top, without hesitation, before I paid my bills, did I gain financial peace and freedom.

I am not going to go out to lunch with Bill Gates or William Buffet, but I don't have to worry about having enough money to go to lunch with a friend who drops in to see me.

> "Bring the whole tithe into the storehouse, that there may be food in my house. Test me in this," says the LORD Almighty, "and see if I will not throw open the floodgates of heaven and pour out so much blessing that there will not be room enough to store it."

Malachi 3:10

Test me in this says the Lord almighty.
**Test me**, he says.

God double dog dares us to try to out give him. He doesn't play fair. He always wins at the giving game. He finds a way to give back to you so much more than you offered to him as your first fruits.

Even among people who have no rental furniture, no costly bad habits, a steady job, health insurance, and all the perks of this 21st century; the family that does not tithe does not have peace. Financially, they are still on the rocks. They do not trust that God will provide.

Worse than not tithing in post modern poverty is the trick tithe.

The what?

The trick tithe. I will trick God into thinking that I am tithing.

There is a hole in my budget. I know that God knows that whatever it is needs to be paid. I will just reroute my tithe to cover than need. College tuition, travel expenses, a more reliable car, and even some charitable causes easily tempt the poverty minded to withhold the tithe in the name of tithing elsewhere.

It works. The trick works. The problem is that it is not God who is tricked. We can trick ourselves, and easily.

When we take God out of the tithing loop, we are saying that our god is not big enough to address our needs unless we redirect our tithe. It's like trading in God for *god minus*. It seems like a good trade at the time. Our version of *god minus* seems to understand our predicament, but only the one true God has challenged us to test him in our tithe.

We wouldn't whittle a god out of wood or chisel one out of stone, but we don't mind shrinking the one true God down to a size where we can negotiate with him. The problem is that God is shrink proof. The god that you got in exchange goes by many names: greed, selfishness, contempt, covetousness, and Lucifer.

Paul writes in his letter to the church in Rome that anything that we do that is not done in faith is sin. How can not trusting God be anything but sin?

*For I have come to turn*

*'a man against his father,*
*a daughter against her mother,*
*a daughter-in-law against her*
*mother-in-law—*
*a man's enemies will be the*
*members of his own household.'*

Matthew 10:35-36

To satisfy selfish desires, families will turn away from God. To circumvent the hard decisions, families will appease their members and turn their backs on God. To feel OK about what they have done, they will make their own gods so they can postpone confessing their apostasy.

All the while, they claim to follow the one true God.

He was not fooled.

## PoMo Poverty

He was not trusted.

He was not tested.

He did not pour out his blessings on those
mocking him.


No other place in the Bible do we see
these words:  **Test me in this**.

So many don't trust.

So many don't test.

So many remain in poverty.


Phones, credit cards, and rental furniture
do not hold a candle to the tithe.  Those
who struggle and tithe have hope because
they trust God and his promises.

Those who do not tithe seldom have hope.
They won't trust.  They are content in
their poverty of distrust.

People don't like to hear it, but the tithe is still a truth-teller when it comes to trusting God.

*Trust in the LORD with all your heart*
*and lean not on your own understanding;*
*in all your ways submit to him,*
*and he will make your paths straight.*

Proverbs 3:5-6

God rewards trust.

No trust.  Know poverty.

Know trust.  No poverty.

## Language

Really?

The poverty of language?

Yes!

> *Neither a borrower nor a lender*
> *be,*
> *For loan oft loses both itself and*
> *friend,*
> *And borrowing dulls the edge of*
> *husbandry.*

> Shakespeare's Hamlet (Act I,
> Scene III)

What happened to the days when words
were both art and science?  What
happened to the well spoken phrase?
What happened to passion and sincerity
in our language?

Now, what do we have?  A text that reads.
"The dog died.  LOL."

So many today can neither read nor write with any skill.  How many people do you know that have not read a book in the last year?  How about in the last 5 years?

How many can even understand the contract they sign to get their cell phone or television service?

How many people do you know that have never memorized a poem, a Bible verse, or even the three lines from Shakespeare noted above?

Much of the poverty of language comes from what takes the place of well formed thoughts.

It includes meaningless catchphrases.

Malaprops of wisdom.

And profanity.

People throw out words and hope that something they say gets them what they want.  They try words and phrases they don't understand and if those don't work, they spice things up a bit with the profane. Coherent, rational, reasoned thought seems to be optional these days.

Ask many people who are struggling today to write out a plan for anything and you would think you had asked them to spit in the grits.

Writing and thinking go hand-in-hand and there is a dearth of both these days.

The post modern world is one of astonishing advances in communication and one of poverty in language.

Tom Spence

*My dear brothers take note of this:*
*Everyone should be quick to listen,*
*slow to speak, and slow to anger, for*
*man's anger does not bring about the*
*righteous life that God desires.*

James 1:19-20

## Time

So many people can't pay their bills, can't find a job, and have more time on their hands than they know what to do with. There should be an oxymoron or two somewhere in that statement.

I have seen a wide range of reactions—from tears to anger so pronounced that veins were about ready to pop out of the person's neck--when I ask someone who is out of work these questions.

How many hours a week do you want to work?

The most popular answer is, "I dunno."

So I respond, "How about 40? That's something of a traditional work week."

Usually, the reply is, "Yeah, OK, that sounds good. Unless I can get some overtime."

So I respond, "How much overtime?"

The answer is predictable, "I dunno."

So I continue with the three questions for one answer game. "How about 20 hours overtime?"

"Yeah, OK, that sounds good. Unless I can get more."

"How much more."

Don't laugh. "I dunno."

"Let's just say another 10 hours. That makes a total of 40 hours regular time and 30 hours overtime. That's 70 hours a week. Can you handle that?"

"Yes."

The affirmative answer should not convey any degree of confidence or commitment. Usually by this point, people are just getting upset that I haven't thrown in the towel and opened the vault of money piled high for people who are out of work and have become exhausted by trying to figure out how much they might be willing to work in a week.

It is at this point where people really don't like me. I say, "You need to spend 70 hours a week looking for a job. Not sitting at home wishing someone would call you with a top level executive job, getting off your butt, hitting the pavement, and finding a job."

The most common response: "Well, I don't have time."

The dichotomy of not having the time to find a job for which one hopes to work at enough be paid overtime seldom registers with the unemployed.

When I say that finding a job is your job until you are hired, you might think that I had said terrible things about the family lineage.

This is poverty.

People have plenty of time to dwell in self pity.

People have no time to help themselves.

Tom Spence

Working as a counselor with inmates, most of whom had several years remaining on their sentences, I learned a term for what so many who live in the poverty of time do. It's called *running your story*.

The inmate with years to do and no place to go will gladly tell you his whole story from the beginning at every chance— except when it's time for chow or recreation. He does not value time, especially yours.

It seems that the unemployed also do not value their time. They have plenty of time to spend with someone who is doing purposeful things, but none to spend looking for a job. They have acquired the art of *running their story*. They value neither their own time nor the time of others.

*Teach us to number our days, that*
*we may gain a heart of wisdom.*

Psalm 90:12

## PoMo Poverty

Each of us are granted 86,400 seconds in a day.

People of purpose cherish each second.

People of poverty just wait for them to pass.


People of purpose realize what they give when they give another person time.

People of poverty neither recognize what time they have nor what time another is giving.


The paradox of poverty is that people, who value time, give it readily for the right reasons.

People, who habitually waste time, seldom engage in productive endeavors. They just don't have the time.

*Tom Spence*

We may have all encountered different obstacles, painful experiences, or had the break of a life time. We don't all start from the same point. Some are ahead or behind others in wealth, education, status, and other measureable areas.

But we all are granted the same amount of time each day.

Purposeful people invest their time.

It is a poverty mindset to waste it.


Want to see the intersection of time and money in the post modern world of poverty?

Go to the convenience store.

Fountain drinks.

Fast food.

Cigarettes.

Energy drinks.

Beer.

And two or three bags of chips.

$35.

That leaves $5 in change. Better get another pack of cigarettes.

Just as well spend it here. The water bill was $52. Didn't have enough to pay it anyway.

I like convenience stores. They are convenient. There is no grocery store in the town where I live, so convenience stores save me the $10 in gas and most of an hour in time to get the one or two items that ran out before my next trip to the grocery store.

People become addicted to the immediate gratification of the convenience store. Many don't even know how to make a shopping list. They just go to the convenience store, and then decide what they need.

*Tom Spence*

Convenience stores are all located at the same place in the land of post modern poverty. They are at the corner of time and money and are irresistible to those who do not know how to value either.

*Time is money.*

Benjamin Franklin

## Stuff

Stuff is no respecter of income.

Stuff clings to the rich.

Stuff clings to those just making it.

Stuff clings to the poor.

Stuff clings to inmates in prison.

Want to ruin an inmate's day? Take his stuff away.

I have seen this time and time again. A security officer takes something of no real value from an inmate, normally because it was against the rules to have it; and the inmate goes bonkers.

You and I would look at the seemingly valueless item and say, "That seems to be valueless."

But it was somebody's stuff. And it was taken away.

*Tom Spence*

How much stuff does a person really need?

Would you think me crazy if I said about 10% of what we actually have?

I have some stuff that I keep for specific purposes.

I have other stuff that I keep because it seems to have general value.

I have other stuff that I keep because it hurts too much to try to remember why I acquired it and why I have kept it this long.

I have some stuff that I keep because as soon as I get rid of it, I will replace it with other stuff.

I don't need any more stuff.

I don't want any more stuff.

I don't want to be owned by my stuff.

I refuse to live in the poverty of stuff.

PoMo Poverty

But stuff is sly.

Stuff is sneaky.

Stuff easily engages the stealth mode.

It finds a way back into your life.

Perhaps in gifts.

Perhaps in buys too good to pass up.

Perhaps in buying something because the
money went to a good cause.


Stuff loves Americans because we love
our stuff.

Most of our stuff does nothing to improve
the quality of our lives.

Perhaps stuff is the status symbol of
poverty.

We can't keep the electricity on, but we
have so much stuff that it fills one or more
rooms.

*Tom Spence*

The poverty of stuff is that it owns us.

If we were truly master in this unsavory relationship, we would kick our stuff to the curb.


People hold onto their stuff longer than they hold onto their marriages.

When marriages dissolve, the stuff gets divided.


But how can we talk of the poverty of stuff? Consider one of the first definitions of poverty that we examined.

> The state or condition of having little or no money, goods, or means of support; condition of being poor. Synonyms: privation, neediness, destitution, indigence, pauperism, penury. Antonyms: riches, wealth, plenty.

Stuff means that you have plenty of "goods" but still lack the means of support. Stuff saps what resources you did have so that despite the fact you can hardly walk through your house because of all of the stuff, you are actually poor.

Perhaps there is an equation for stuff and poverty. I suspect it to be an inverse relationship. The more stuff you have, the deeper you are into poverty. The less stuff that has attached itself to you, the greater your chances of escaping the prison of poverty.

Many are imprisoned in poverty by their stuff.

There is a subset of stuff known as tubs.

Tubs let us sort our stuff so that it appears to have purpose.

Tubs postpone the day when we have to buy a storage shed for our stuff.

Tubs efficiently store stuff. You can stack tubs to the ceiling where otherwise it could only be piled 5 or 6 feet high.

Tubs rescue us from breaking out of poverty. They let us keep our stuff longer. They postpone the inevitable a little longer.

Tubs keep us from seeing our stuff as our master for another year, two years, or maybe even a decade.

Sometimes the stuff inside the tubs is worthless, but tubs make it easier to keep more worthless stuff.

Many are imprisoned in poverty by their stuff. Tubs reduce the possibility of early release.

## Character

Does being poor in character make one poor in the world?

Not always, but that's the way to bet.

Some would say that poor decisions are what make people poor.

There is some truth in that.

But biblical proverbs might differ.

*Better to be poor and honest than rich and dishonest.*

Proverbs 28:6 (Good News Bible)

*Bloodthirsty people hate anyone who's honest, but righteous people will protect the life of such a person.*

Proverbs 29:10 (Good News Bible)

Could honest people, men and women of integrity, end up poor?

Yes, but they would surely not be in poverty. Their character intact, poverty cannot consume them.

Again, let us consider one of the definitions of poverty.

The state of being inferior in quality or insufficient in amount.

Poor is not necessarily destitute. Poor is not always starving. Sometimes poor is just enough to get by.

The man or woman of character surely is not inferior in quality. And what does it mean to be insufficient in amount? We just considered the poverty of stuff.

So if you can be poor and still have character, what is the poverty of character?

Perhaps the poverty of character might better be described as the comfort of poverty. There is a certain degree of comfort in poverty.

You can be a victim. You are not responsible. Someone else needs to address any real issues with regard to your life.

You feel no obligation to change the way you live. If it's not your fault, then why should you have to be the one to change?

You can live nearly risk free. There is risk in change. Risk involves some responsibility. Risk involves addressing fear. That takes character. Some choose not to change—to remain in a pitiful state—instead of to take what they do have and take a chance to improve.

Consider the lessons in this parable of Jesus.

### The Parable of the Talents

*"Again, it will be like a man going on a journey, who called his*

servants and entrusted his property to them. To one he gave five talents of money, to another two talents, and to another one talent, each according to his ability. Then he went on his journey. The man who had received the five talents went at once and put his money to work and gained five more. So also, the one with the two talents gained two more. But the man who had received the one talent went off, dug a hole in the ground and hid his master's money.

"After a long time the master of those servants returned and settled accounts with them. The man who had received the five talents brought the other five. 'Master,' he said, 'you entrusted me with five talents. See, I have gained five more.'

"His master replied, 'Well done, good and faithful servant! You have been faithful with a few things; I will put you in charge of many things. Come and share your master's happiness!'

"The man with the two talents also came. 'Master,' he said, 'you entrusted me with two talents; see, I have gained two more.'

"His master replied, 'Well done, good and faithful servant! You have been faithful with a few things; I will put you in charge of many things. Come and share your master's happiness!'

"Then the man who had received the one talent came. 'Master,' he said, 'I knew that you are a hard man, harvesting where you have not sown and gathering where you have not scattered seed. So I was afraid and went out and hid your talent in the ground. See, here is what belongs to you.'

*"His master replied, 'You wicked, lazy servant! So you knew that I harvest where I have not sown and gather where I have not scattered seed? Well then, you should have put my money on deposit with the bankers, so that when I returned I would have received it back with interest.*

*"'Take the talent from him and give it to the one who has the ten talents. For everyone who has will be given more, and he will have an abundance. Whoever does not have, even what he has will be taken from him. And throw that worthless servant outside, into the darkness, where there will be weeping and gnashing of teeth.'"*

Matthew 25:14-30 NIV

We all must ask ourselves a question. It's the same question for all of us. It's one that we expect God to ask us one day.

## PoMo Poverty

What did you do with what I gave you?

What did you do with what I gave you?

What did you do with what I gave you?


Men and women of character ask
themselves this question daily.  Those
who live in the poverty of character
cringe at the day it will be asked of them.


Notice in the parable how the third
servant comes to the master and just
starts spewing out excuses.  It is as if the
rapid fire excuse mode will do away with
the question.

I see this every week.

At church.

At Walmart.

At the ball game.

At the gas pump.

People whom the church has helped—
often on more than one occasion—see me
and are afraid to begin a conversation
with "hello, howdy, how are you" or any
conventional greeting.  They must launch
into their excuses for fear I might ask:

Did you finish that budget?

Did you pay your water bill or buy
cigarettes?

Did you think to put your clothes outside
to air out so the smell of marijuana wasn't
so distinct?

How did that credit card fraud thing turn
out?

I never ask these things.  I only ask, "How
have you been?"  That is, if I get a chance
to speak.  But it is apparent that the
excuse defense condition for those poor
in character is always set at DefCon 4.

The poverty of character is that people must carry around ready-made excuses holstered at their side in case they must be drawn out quickly.

The poverty of character is that people dread answering the question we all must answer someday. What did you do with what I gave you?

The poverty of character is that after spewing out this irrational babble so many times, people actually start to believe it.

If you are not going to try to do the right thing, if you are not going to try to better yourself, if you are not going to risk what you do have—time, talents, abilities, physical strength, or anything else that God blessed you with—then one excuse is as good as another. Really one is as bad as another.

To live in the poverty of character is to miss out on life altogether. It's not to play it safe. It is not to play at all.

*It is not the critic who counts; not the man who points out how the strong man stumbles, or where the doer of deeds could have done them better. The credit belongs to the man who is actually in the arena, whose face is marred by dust and sweat and blood; who strives valiantly; who errs, who comes short again and again, because there is no effort without error and shortcoming; but who does actually strive to do the deeds; who knows great enthusiasms, the great devotions; who spends himself in a worthy cause; who at the best knows in the end the triumph of high achievement, and who at the worst, if he fails, at least fails while daring greatly, so that his place shall never be with those cold and timid souls who neither know victory nor defeat.*

Theodore Roosevelt from the speech "Citizenship In A Republic", delivered at the Sorbonne,

Paris, France on 23 April, 1910

## PoMo Poverty

Men and women of low character are
pitiful creatures. They won't trust God.
They don't trust themselves, and anyone
who knows them surely won't trust them.


The poverty of character is perhaps the
most painful form of poverty of all.

Tom Spence

*By the Eternal! There is a man whose form should be cast in deathless bronze and the statue placed in every college of the land. It is not book-learning young men need, nor instruction about this and that, but a stiffening of the vertebrae which will cause them to be loyal to a trust, to act promptly, concentrate their energies: do the thing - "Carry a message to Garcia!"*

Elbert Hubbard

"A Message To Garcia"

## Commitment

Commitment is the kissing cousin of character.

They are different enough to deserve separate discussions, but somewhere up the line the family tree is rooted in the same place.

I knew that things would be different once I left the Marine Corps. Still, there was some culture shock. Perhaps the greatest came in the area of commitment.

In the Corps, if you said you would do a thing, you did it.

If you said you would be at a certain place at a certain time, you were there.

If another counted on you for his very life, his life was in good hands.


In the world, any old excuse seems good enough not to honor a commitment.

"I will absolutely have that for you by close of business today. I won't go home until it's done. On my honor, it will be done."

Who says things like this?

Generally, people who do not honor their commitments. Jesus said, *let your **yes** be **yes** and your **no** be **no**.*

People of commitment, don't commit to things casually.

They consider what they commit themselves to do.

Their **yes** is **yes**.

They seldom feel a need to explain their no.

When you get a **yes**, it is a **yes**. No amplifying verbiage is required or will be given.

"I will absolutely have that for you by close of business today. I won't go home until it's done. On my honor, it will be done." Here are some typical answers when the thing promised is not done.

*Something came up.*

*I got a call.*

*The boss needed me.*

*I forgot.*

*Go figure.*

The word "commitment" in the Corps meant commitment. In the world at large, it too often means "if it is convenient." Actually, "if it is convenient and I happen to remember without too much effort" might be a little closer.

The dedication required to change or improve something in one's own life is lacking in much of today's world.

Efficacy is the power to produce desired change. I most often use this term with drug addicts, those with criminal thinking patterns, and those who don't want to be powerless in their own lives any more.

Where there is no commitment, there is no efficacy.

*That which we obtain too easily, we esteem too lightly.*

Thomas Paine

## Fear

God did not give us a spirit of fear.

To live with fear as a companion in our lives is to live with less than we should have.

It is to live with less than God desires for us.

God gives us courage.

God gives us self-discipline.

God gives us truth.

God gives us hope.

Fear saps the life right out of life.


Fear is poverty.

Courage brings abundance.


God gives us courage and we are to encourage each other.

Without courage, we cannot enjoy abundance even when we seem to have an abundance.

We learn fear early.

Consider our children as they get in line. Our youngest know these words: **No cuts!**

If someone gets in front of you, there might be less for you.  Fear governs.

**No cuts!**

This isn't life or death fear, but we often act like it is.

This isn't innate fear that tells us, *far enough*, as we lean over the edge to look at the ground from the top of a 40 story building.

This is fear based in selfishness.

**_There might be less for me or if I can get there first, I might get more._**

Consider the Black Friday sales. Before the days when many of the big stores were open 24 hours, people would camp out overnight to buy a VCR for $39. Had they waited another two months, they could have bought it at regular price for $29.

Fear has moved many a merchant from the red to the black. People still bite on these post-Thanksgiving sales. You may not need what is on sale, but the thought of everyone else having one and you left out is unbearable.

We should stop periodically and ask ourselves, _Would I make this decision if I wasn't afraid?_

We have to get over the initial thought process that tells us we are not afraid and do some real searching. Why are we making this decision?

If we can get to the point where we can see fear at work, we can also see the poverty that it creates.

~

*This is preeminently the time to speak the truth, the whole truth, frankly and boldly. Nor need we shrink from honestly facing conditions in our country today. This great Nation will endure as it has endured, will revive and will prosper. So, first of all, let me assert my firm belief that the only thing we have to fear is fear itself—nameless, unreasoning, unjustified terror which paralyzes needed efforts to convert retreat into advance. In every dark hour of our national life a leadership of frankness and vigor has met with that understanding and support of the people themselves which is essential to victory.*

Franklin Delano Roosevelt

First Inaugural Address

## Purpose

The Germans have a unique word:
*Gestalt.*

It is a word that is used to say the whole is more than the sum of its parts.

It describes an integral relationship among all elements.

It's more than integrity.

It is integrity plus synergy with a fully intertwined taxonomy.

OK, let's just go with the whole is more than the sum of the parts.


How can something be more than the sum of its component parts?

In the world of life experience, purpose is often the cohesive, the organizing principle, and the multiplier.

A life expended with purpose is a life lived beyond its potential.

Purpose gets you out of bed in the morning.

Purpose causes you to say, *Good Morning, Lord*, instead of *Good Lord, it's morning.*

Purpose gets you to school

Purpose gets you to work.

Purpose gets you talking with God.

Purpose gets you up the hill.

Purpose lets the insult roll off while focus is maintained.

Purpose adjusts the sails when the wind changes.

Purpose cooks Ramen when the paycheck isn't enough for the water bill.

Purpose crosses the minefield to save a friend.

Purpose gives insight into our Heavenly Father.

Purpose gives us insight into ourselves.

Purpose unlocks our gifts and talents.

Purpose gives us permission to say **no** to things we don't need to do.

Purpose brings us to abundance—not in stuff or money—but in life.

Purpose purges poverty.

Those who live without purpose endure a cruel type of poverty.

This form of poverty just passes the time.

This form of poverty sees only immediate needs.

Character atrophies in those living in the poverty of purpose.

Commitment is foreign to anyone without purpose.

The power to effect desired change is irrelevant if there is no desire.

*Tom Spence*

Fear rules.

Language sours.

Money is illusive.

There is no Sabbath to take in a life
without purpose.


People without purpose are often deluded
into thinking they have purpose or a plan
or at least a general approach to life.
What we most often find is that they have
an exact set of circumstances that they
are looking for before they will pursue
anything.

What circumstances?

Something that pays a lot, requires little,
and doesn't require any commitment.


People without purpose are often deluded
into thinking that they can do anything
that comes along. Sure, they can be a
manager, or salesperson, or inventory

specialist. They won't show up to apply because that would shatter the delusion.

People without purpose gravitate to infomercials. Something priced at $29.95 in which you get 2, not 1, of the save-your-life item offers allure. When you have no purpose, anything that glitters must be gold.

People with purpose enjoy a good conversation but can't pause for long.

People without purpose love to talk all day but are terrible conversationalists.

People with purpose love to engage others who will challenge their thinking.

People without purpose avoid thinking.

People without purpose avoid life.

People without purpose feel cheated out of something.

They have cheated themselves out of life.

People of purpose arrive at the job site thinking, *what can I accomplish?*

People without purpose arrive reluctantly at their job wondering when the day will end.

People of purpose are amazed at how fast the day passes.

People without purpose are tortured by the never-ending day.


People with purpose seize the day.

People living in the poverty of purpose dread the day.


It is a pitiful sight to see a human void of purpose.

There is no life in the eyes.

There is no spring in the step.

There is no confidence in the voice.

## PoMo Poverty

There is no firmness in the handshake.

There is no place to go to find peace.

There is no hope to carry this miserable
person to a better place.


What a burden to carry—to exist without
reason.

What a burden to believe that you have
no purpose.


What a burden to be blind to the truth.

God made us all with purpose.

Living without purpose is not natural.

Living without purpose is to reject God.


Purpose is part of life.

Purpose is integral to abundant life.

Tom Spence

Purpose pervades life and gives no purchase to poverty.

Yet I deal with people every week who make life decisions in an instant, and postpone simple decisions for months or years.

I meet with people that come seeking money to pay a bill with no idea of what they will do to pay the bill next month, much less what they want to do with their lives.

My skin crawls when people come to me and say, *well I guess we'll get married.* It was as if they were choosing between Ziploc bag sizes. *Yeah, OK, that one will work.*

I have mixed thoughts when some people without purpose come and tell me that they are leaving town. *Something happened at the school. We can't stay here. No teacher is going to correct my child.*

I get blank stares when I ask, *why is your child in school?*

People literally cannot answer this question. Maybe if they said: *so she can get an education, or so he can learn something,* or something along the lines of *so they can better themselves;* then an honest discussion might be possible.

But when there is no purpose—or the parents do not comprehend the purpose and just go along with the crowd— discussions about staying the course, learning discipline, and reinforcing the rules set by the teacher are bad subtitles on a foreign film.

I said that I had mixed thoughts about people without purpose leaving town. Among the other thoughts are *which of my contemporaries should I warn as the people of poverty head their way.*


Purpose is part of life.

Purpose is integral to abundant life.

Tom Spence

Purpose pervades life and gives no
purchase to poverty.

And yet so many will have nothing to do
with purpose in their lives.

*A ship is safe in harbor, but that's not
what ships are for.*

William Shedd

## 24/7

Only those in the most remote parts of America don't know what 24/7 is. They have grown up with it for at least two decades. A world where you had to wait until morning to get a new pair of jeans is foreign to anyone under 20.

There are many blessings to having everything available all the time. Surely no one should have to wait until morning to get things that you can't live without, such as earphones for you IPod or the perfect pair of shoes to go with the dress that you want to wear in the morning.

What could be wrong with a never ending buffet to satisfy our always hungry consumer appetite?

What's the problem with immediate gratification?

What's the problem with 24/7?

Other than, it has created a society without a Sabbath?

The poverty of 24/7 goes beyond retailers.

Long ago and far away, I was a second lieutenant with my first assignment to a Fleet Marine Force unit. I was stationed at Camp Schwab in Okinawa, Japan. It was a long way from small town Oklahoma. That was just the way I wanted it. I wanted to see the world.

I carried a thin, standard issue, 3 X 5 olive drab notebook. When the company commander had a meeting, you made some notes. These notes translated into tasks for your Marines. The small notebook was sufficient. You paid attention, made the notes you needed, and got the job done. It was just that simple.

Today, it seems that nothing can take place without handouts, web links, presentations, and catch phrases.

Information comes at us so fast that we seldom remember even the most important things that we need to do, not do, or otherwise be cognizant of.

I often promulgate information in church bulletins, handouts, via blogs and Facebook, via online articles, and also on the church website. This is complemented by numerous verbal announcements at a series of gatherings.

Still people will ask me, **When is that thing?**

Information is everywhere so we seldom latch onto anything we consider important and make a note.

Here is the anomaly in the 24/7 system. Everyone who is alive today has always had 24/7 access to The Bible. It remains closed 24/7 in most homes.

Sometimes it is open because it is a display item, like a decorative candle stand.

If there is trouble of any kind, people are more likely to go to Walmart than to open the Bible. Walmart is already open. You have to open the Bible yourself.

The ultimate 24/7 crusader is the television and its first cousin the internet. Somewhere in this family is the adopted son, the video game. Sometimes they all get together and people can play video games connected to the internet and displayed on the big screen TV.

Most people under 20 have never seen a test pattern, heard the National Anthem played on the tube unless it was at the beginning of a sporting event, and have never known a time when television was not a 24/7 entity.

One or more of these three likely steal several hours each week from your life. Some may surrender several hours each day.

This is not the two or three well written shows for which the family gathers and enjoys together. It is not checking the new pictures of the grandkids uploaded to the web by your kids. It is not the hour set aside to play a digital game as part of a real recreation experience. These are blessings of technology.

It is to be sleep deprived after watching reruns all night. It is to be nearly brain dead at work from chatting with someone you don't know about things that don't matter into the wee hours of the morning. It is to be too exhausted from saving the planet from ungodly online invaders to take the kids to school or even to notice that you have kids.

The time that we spend loving our children is truly an eternal investment. Time wasted in front of the tube or its relatives is an infernal divestment.

We always have 24/7 access to something.

Our family.

Our thoughts.

The Bible.

Walmart.

Television.

Internet.

Video Games.

God.


For people who claim to love the one true God, it is strange that the Creator of 24/7 access is often relegated to a few quips at meal times.

OK, sometimes if we are in big trouble, we will check in a few more times.


Sometimes we worry a lot and count this as prayer. News Flash: **That dog don't hunt!**

Worry is worry and prayer is prayer. You can't substitute salt for sugar in most recipes and you can't substitute worry for prayer and expect good things to come to you.

The poverty of 24/7 is that God is always available to us, yet we choose the temporary things of the world instead.

The poverty of 24/7 is that God told us to observe a special time of rest and thinking about him. We chose non-stop busyness and coveting what the world has instead.

What good is it to gain the entire world and yet lose our soul?

Tom Spence

*What good will it be for a man if he gains the whole world, yet forfeits his soul? Or what can a man give in exchange for his soul?*

Matthew 16:26 (NIV)

## Efficacy

Efficacy is the power to effect desired change.

It is doing what needs to be done to make real, substantial change in our lives.

The poverty of efficacy is the most debilitating of all. Where there is no will or ability to make change, there is no hope.

Christians know that with God everything is possible. Many learned that the hard way. Many built upon their own success. All eventually crash. All eventually understand that a house build upon a sand foundation will not weather the storm.

With God, we know we can change.

We can stop smoking.

We can get up an hour earlier and exercise.

We can take a class and hold down our job.

We can take care of our family and better ourselves.

We can give up 90% of the television that we watch for something better, including reading the Bible, prayer, service to others, and just being still.

You can make changes that you desire without having God first in your life. They will just be temporary changes. There is no shortage of programs and tools. I know people who have lost a hundred pounds in a year. The fact that they gained them all back and then some shows they can do it, but that they can't really make the desired change stick.

The poverty of self efficacy is often visible in vocabulary.

*I tried that.*

*I can't do that.*

*It doesn't work for me.*

*Nobody can do that.*

*It's just too hard.*

Without the power to effect the changes we desire, we feel like victims. We see ourselves as victims in every situation. Any new experience is just another chance to be a victim.

People that can't hold down a job often hold onto some key phrases.

*If my boss isn't a jerk...*

*If they don't mess with my schedule...*

*If they give me enough overtime...*

*If they don't expect me to work overtime...*

*If they let me do things my way...*

Here are a few that mean the same thing but are proffered with a feigned optimism.

*I'll give it a try.*

*I will try my best.*

*I'll give it a shot.*

*I will see what happens.*

These translate to, *I already have my excuses lined up for when I have to quit because of something that happened only to me.*

The person living with the poverty of efficacy is defeated before he begins because that's the way he wants it. To take on the challenges of a new job means forsaking the comfort of being a victim. If you get the sorry end of the stick at your new job, you are prepared to walk away. Your life is a mess but your excuses are in order.

People with self efficacy negotiate the more difficult assignments, the bottom of the totem pole tasks, and the fact that they are the *new guy* until they are not. It's not an ideal world, but it is the world in which they live and are called upon to use their resourcefulness to overcome its imperfections.

These people are seldom the *new guy* for long. They stick things out until they earn the respect of their peers and seniors. They see many hired after them return to the comfort of being an unemployed victim.

We see this far too often in marriages these days. Consider the verbiage that often comes up at the corner of commitment and efficacy with people who struggle in their marriages.

*If I am going to stay with him...*

*If we decide to stay together...*

*If we decide we need Christ in our marriage...*

Tom Spence

*When he starts bringing home more money...*

*When she starts listening to me...*

These statements are generally followed by some action.

*Then I will stop drinking...*

*Then I will quit smoking...*

*Then I will read to my kids...*

*Then I will hold down a job...*

*Then I will go back to school...*

*Then I will start going to church...*

*Then I will do something that I already have the power to do on my own but my spouse is my current excuse for not doing it.*

Mix and match the above lists as desired. The fact that most people who live in the land of self efficacy can spot the disconnect from the first condition and the second doesn't register on people who perceive themselves as victims. They have a ready-made excuse when they are confronted with the absurdity of these statements.

*You're judging me!*

There is sometimes a very fine line between judging and speaking the truth.

How do you know on which side of the line you stand?

Love.

Love won't condemn.

Love compels you to speak the truth.

Love doesn't say, *I told you so.*

Love feels the hurt of the other person and longs to help.

Sometimes that help is not money.

Sometimes that help is truth.

*But I live in poverty! Of course I need money!*

There is no argument in that statement. How to come by the needed currency and use it effectively are often a very extended discussion. They are a discussion avoided most of the time with one phrase.

*You're judging me!*

Let us for the sake of argument say that such a statement is true. Does that change anything?

Does the fact that others are judging you change your condition?

I engaged in this discussion hundreds of times with inmates. You ask, *what do you want?*

Some version of this follows.

*I want to get out and stay out of prison. I'll do whatever it takes.*

Some meant it. Some did it. Some fully grasped efficacy.

And some were coming back within months if not days or weeks of their release. They wanted out but would not do what was needed to change the way they lived. Their words said one thing. Their behavior said another. The discussion usually revolved around fairness.

*That's not fair.*

*That officer doesn't like me.*

*He's always picking on me.*

*That's not what they did to everyone else.*

*The system is not fair.*

The fairness in question could be anything from having a parole hearing postponed 24 hours to someone cutting in the chow line. Sometimes the complaints were absolutely true.

My response generally went along these lines.

*Will getting what you want in this situation—to never come back to this place again—get you closer to that goal?*

The first few times that I worked with an inmate, the response was generally, **No but...**

What a truth telling combination: **No but**.

What I am asking for won't really help me with my biggest priority.

But my biggest priority isn't really my biggest priority.

Then what is?

**Not having to change. If anything needs to change, it's the world I live in.**

Therein resides the poverty of efficacy.

Fairness and effectiveness often work in opposition to each other.

Marines are the best marksmen on the planet. They qualify annually with their assigned weapons. Marines shoot at small targets from long distances. Wind impacts the trajectory of a round. The greater the wind, the greater the adjustment that a Marine must make with his settings.

One group qualifies one week with clear skies, comfortable temperatures, and almost no wind. Next week another group contends with some drizzle, a chill in the air, and high winds. That's hardly fair, is it?

Perhaps not, but it is effective. Marines do not always engage the enemy on their own schedule. Sometimes the weather is hot and the wind blows without fail. Other days are cold—bone chilling cold. Still other days are better suited for a backyard cookout in shorts and tee shirts with good conversation around meat roasting over an open flame.

Marines are called to serve and fight in all.

It doesn't seem fair, but it is effective.

The Marine finds a way to hit the target whether it is made of paper and cloth or assorted terrorist parts. He is not concerned about being fair. He is just going to hit his target.

What's not fair is being on the other end of this deal without a white flag nearby.


I dealt with some young men who were always needing help and never willing to help themselves. I asked them if they were happy with their situation.

The more vocal of the two said yes. He continued that he did not want anymore meddling in his family's business.

A few weeks later, he was asking everyone for help with his car. That's not quite true. He was rudly demanding that people fix his vehicle.

When he came to see me I asked, *I thought you were happy with your situation.*

He said, *I am. I'm just not happy with my transportation situation.*

The translation to *povertyspeak* is: *I am happy with my situation unless I need more than everyone will give me without any effort on my part.*

Had this young man spent as much time doing odd jobs for cash as he did complaining how unfair everyone was being towards him, he could have hired someone to fix his car and gone back to his do-nothing life.

He would invest none of his own effort in himself.

After just over 20 years in the Marine Corps, I retired.

I was not going to be promoted again.

Of the few hundred officers in my year group, I think one was promoted beyond me. Many of my contemporaries left the Corps about the same time. Things had changed. The Corps was forced to comply with federal law that set timeframes for promotion. For most of my career, the Corps simply did not comply with this. I was caught in a time of transition.

Could I have done something to change this? Could I have done something to increase my chances for promotion?

Probably. I could have lobbied for more time in a combat zone. I could have run 10 miles per day instead of 7. I could have been more tactful and less truthful. I could have sought more high profile assignments.

I did not. I was not driven to live for promotion. I was satisfied with the career I had been given. I was the beneficiary of too many experiences that I can only classify as **abundant** to complain about how far I had or had not gone. I left the Corps without regrets.

And I accept the fact that others may have been more qualified to command regiments and divisions than I was.

I truly loved leading, teaching, serving, and working with Marines. I could have been more driven to achieve more for myself, but that would not be consistent with who I am.

I embrace the fact that in my lifetime, I received another more profound calling.

The power to effect change in my life has always been there. Some things were worth making sacrifices and changes in order to become what I desired.

Other things did not carry the same attraction or purpose.

Everything that I have set my heart and mind upon, I have achieved. It is nothing to boast about. God provided me with the things I needed.

He equipped me not only with the means to achieve these goals, but the goals themselves.

I am blessed with efficacy.

I don't have to worry about challenges.

My yes can be yes and my no is no.

I love to begin new challenges, revise the method and mode, try again, improve, revise, review and revise again. I love to take the gifts, talents, abilities that God has given me and see what I can do with them. I am not afraid to venture into areas that are new to me.

I may not know what I am getting into, but I know me.

And I hurt when I see the poverty of efficacy played out before me each day.

God has and will continue to empower us to do exactly what we need to do to live a full life. It is painful to watch people retreat to the comfort of being a victim time and time again.

It just hurts to watch knowing that but in the rarest of circumstances, these people are equipped to change their lives.

It just hurts.

Tom Spence

*Jesus looked hard at them and said, "No chance at all if you think you can pull it off yourself. Every chance in the world if you trust God to do it."*

Matthew 19:26 (*The Message*)

## What can we do?

For those who truly walk in the Spirit,
efficacy has become a lifelong companion.
Retreating to a comfort zone in
Victimsville is repulsive.  We are blessed
not to remember the way back there.

But so many live there.

They live in poverty of all sorts.

Some get out.

Most get comfortable with being a victim
of their own lives.

What can we do?


Giving money both helps and hurts.

Sometimes we are called to meet a basic
need without regard for long term
consequences.

Sometimes we are called to speak the
truth and disperse no cash.

Truth is liberating.

Truth can also be difficult to swallow, especially if one has spent a lifetime avoiding it.

Therefore, we must speak the truth in love.

The wisdom on this matter says:

Truth without love is dogma.

Love without truth is hypocrisy.

We are called to speak the truth in love.

Love does not dilute the truth.

The rich young ruler whom Jesus loved was also given instruction that was hard to swallow. *Go sell all that you have, give the money to the poor, and come follow me.* The young man went away sad.

When Jesus told the woman caught in adultery that he did not condemn her but that she must sin no more, these were life-changing instructions. Being on the verge of being stoned is a Significant Emotional Event, but the emotion would wear off. The words of Jesus would not. The woman was directed to change her life.

These two are surely a model for speaking the truth in love. Both people needed to make big changes. Both were given their directions directly from Jesus.

Neither person was condemned in their weakness but the truth was offered full strength to both people.

We who do not live in poverty are required to speak the truth.

The truth is that there is a better way to live.

The truth is that without God, whatever help is offered will be futile.

The truth is that it takes courage to speak the truth.

If speaking the truth to another person about something in their lives does not take courage, it is because it is not offered in love. The truth spoken in judgment doesn't take courage. It takes contempt.

Contempt has set many an ambush near the truth.

We set out to speak the truth in love, but somehow condemn the person at the other end of the conversation. It's not logical. People living in poverty have nothing that we want.

Many of their actions are contemptible. *I've earned my disability and shouldn't have to work* causes my skin to crawl every time I hear it. I must remind myself that even though this person has somehow manipulated the system, I don't want any part of his lifestyle. He has nothing for me to envy. She has nothing for me to covet. The family lives in poverty.

In fact, I really don't want to even speak with these people. In many cases their actions are probably fraudulent or criminal.

Only love would compel us to work with people who don't care that when they beat the system, we who work within the system are the ones who pay for their narcotics of poverty.

Only love would cause us to work through difficult conversations time and time again until finally people accept that they have been living a lie or they just stop coming back.

Speaking the truth in love is the first step.

The second is like it. Living the truth in love. We have to be willing to mentor people who finally want to live in the truth instead of in poverty. This must be done in love and with love.

Mentoring involves words like, *follow me.*

*Let me show you.*

*Let me help you.*

Tom Spence

*Let's do this together.*

*We will figure it out.*

Mentoring involves more than speaking the truth. It involves loving the truth and each other. To throw someone a Bible and say, *Get after it*, may seem like we have done something; but truly we have just said, *Get back to where you belong. Go back to poverty.*

In one of my recent pontifications, <u>Throw Away Kids</u>, I proffer that we who have successfully transited the parenting gauntlet along with those keeping their heads above water now, must lead and mentor those who have given up. Many may not think that they are qualified. Many parents remember only their mistakes, not how they bounced back after making a miscue and returned as a stronger parent.

## PoMo Poverty

Much like mentoring others to be parents, we sometimes do not feel qualified to lead others out of poverty.

We are qualified.

Without exception, I contend that all of us have known poverty in some form.

Even the very rich succumb to the poverty of fear.

Character is not tied to income level.

Time proceeds forward and stuff clings to all socio-economic levels.

All of us contend with a society without a Sabbath.


Yet in this century, some have escaped these ubiquitous forms of Post Modern Poverty.

We are not experts, but we are qualified as guides.

*Tom Spence*

We may not be wealthy by the world's standards, but we are rich towards God.

We are also those whom have been given much and from whom much is expected.

We are to lead our neighbors out of poverty.

## Towards Abundance

It is not enough to lead someone out of a place. There must also be a destination.

Do we lead people out of poverty only to leave them on the precipice of relapse?

Do we lead them to a destination called average or mediocre?


We lead them to where we live.

We lead them to abundance.

We lead them to a life of love and charity.

We lead them to Jesus.

We lead them to life.


Those who follow us as we follow Christ are to exit poverty and enter life.

We are to enjoy life to the full.

We are to lead others to this fullness.

## Abundant Life

What is it to have life to the full?

What is it to fully live?

*To trust the one True God.*

Instead of the obvious ways of the world.

In spite of the alluring ways of the world.

*To live with purpose.*

A God given purpose.

An irresistible purpose.

*To live with passion.*

A God given passion.

An irresistible passion.

## PoMo Poverty

*To become love.*

As God is love.

As he made us to be love.


*To live in obedience to God.*

Instead of to our selfish nature.

And understand our freedom to truly live.


*To number our days.*

And realize the incredible value of life.

Value that atrophies when not used.


*To enter life.*

Not as existence as the world defines life.

But in divine relationship as God has defined it.

Tom Spence

*To fully live.*

Seizing every moment of our existence.

Realizing that the fullness we know now
will seem miniscule in the age to come.


To live abundantly is to live trusting,
obeying, purposefully, passionately, as
God's love in this world for however
many days we have been given and to
know that there is much more to come.

## And Back to Paradox

What is the opposite of poverty?

Wealth?

Let's go with abundance instead.


Isn't abundance wealth?

Not always, in fact, abundance may exist
more frequently without wealth.


The Philippine family with the pool table
inside the cardboard house probably
lived an abundant life. They had adequate
provision and seemed to value the time
they had together. A company of Marines
in full combat gear was something to
watch but not to fear. They were living.


Escaping poverty and living abundantly is
best gauged not by how much we have
but by how much we give.

Tom Spence

If we hoard, cling to our stuff, are afraid to risk anything, fret away our time, and must meet our every desire right now, then we live in poverty regardless of our income.

If we freely give of our time, money, and possessions then we are free from poverty.

Our money, things, time, language serve us as we serve God.

Selfish temptations give into purposeful living time and time again.

We have the God-given power to effect the desired changes in our lives.

These most often come not by serving ourselves but by serving others.

We understand fullness in giving fully more than we do in getting something for ourselves.

Poverty is holding onto everything and losing life.

Abundance is letting go and entering life.

When we hold on for too long, our time, money, things, and fear have hold of us.

When we let go on a regular basis, God places the things of this world at our disposal.

Everyone says, *You can't take it with you.*

Poverty says, *C'mon, give it a try. Hold on to as much as you can for as long as you can even if it kills you.*

Those who are freed from poverty don't miss the stuff they used to cling to.

People living abundantly, give of their time to good causes.

People living abundantly give their words to others with care as if dispensing life-saving medicine.

People living abundantly would not give up their character for anything in the world. What good is it to gain the whole world and lose your soul?

People living abundantly face the same fears that those in poverty face. They just don't give them a home. Our hope is in the Lord. God does not give us a spirit of fear. He grants us courage.

People living abundantly pray without ceasing. Their very lives are a conversation with God. They understand 24/7 better than any merchant.

People living abundantly understand that it is more blessed to give than to receive.

People living abundantly understand that we are free only when we live in the truth.

People living abundantly embrace the power to make desired change.

People living abundantly know—don't
suspect or wish—they know that with
God all things are possible.

People living abundantly are people of
mercy.

They hurt when they see others addicted
to poverty.

They hurt so much they can only say,
*follow me.*

God told his people when they entered
the Promised Land that there should be
no poor among them. He was giving them
all they needed to take care of each other.

Jesus said that we will always have the
poor among us.

These statements are not in conflict.

We—especially in this very blessed
nation—should have no poor among us.

_Tom Spence_

We have the means to meet everyone's needs.

But we still have the poor.  We still have poverty.  We have become pitiful.

We are pitiful because we have the means to live as a nation of communities in which there is no poverty.

We are pitiful because we have too often chosen to place blame instead of placing our lives before God as a living sacrifice.

We are pitiful because we have given money, food, and clothing without love.

We have thrown resources at poverty without the courage to lead people out of poverty to real life.

Long ago in a place named the Marine Corps Recruit Depot, Parris Island, South Carolina I was introduced to a simple phrase.

_Another opportunity to excel._

It usually followed some nearly insane task I had been given by my battalion commander, James Livingston. He was a lieutenant colonel at the time and I was a lieutenant. Normally, if the battalion commander had something special he wanted you to do, you reported to his office.

If it was something out of left field with minimal chance of success, he found you, put his hand on your shoulder and said:

> *OK Tiger, it's just another*
> *opportunity to excel!*

No written orders would accompany the personal message. You just knew it was time to muster every gift, talent, ability, and ounce of creativity you had to accomplish the task.

Today, we who live full lives have another opportunity to excel.

We have an insurmountable problem that goes by the name of poverty, entitlement, victim mindset, and lack of self efficacy.

It manifests itself in different forms in this new century, but its family tree includes such names as fear, lies, selfishness, profanity, hopelessness, and waste.

We who have been delivered from poverty are called to accept that God has placed us in this very time. This is our era. This is our age.

Poverty is our challenge.

Poverty is our opportunity to excel.


We are called to lead people to today's promised land of abundance.

Leaving this to another generation is to walk away from our calling.

Leaving this to the government alone is to walk away from our commission.

Leaving so many behind in poverty is unthinkable.

We must have the courage to give of ourselves to lead others to give of themselves and in the process leave the world of poverty for the land of abundance.

This is our calling.

Tom Spence

*God knew what he was doing from the very beginning. He decided from the outset to shape the lives of those who love him along the same lines as the life of his Son. The Son stands first in the line of humanity he restored. We see the original and intended shape of our lives there in him. After God made that decision of what his children should be like, he followed it up by calling people by name. After he called them by name, he set them on a solid basis with himself. And then, after getting them established, he stayed with them to the end, gloriously completing what he had begun.*

Romans 8:29-30 (*The Message*)

# The Abundance of Inclusion

*Koinonia*

Poverty comes down to a lack of fellowship.

Those enslaved by poverty may be victims of an entitlement mentality, lack of character and courage, their aversion to commitment, or just feeling comfortable as a victim. Those are surely among the leading causes of poverty in the land of opportunity.

All causes share one thing in common. People in poverty are part of the *out group.* They are not part of the family.

If someone in the family hits hard times, the family takes care of him.

If someone in the family truly has a run of bad luck, the family cares for her.

If a family in the family is hurting, the family comforts the family.

Why are they not part of the family?

Sometimes those in poverty have been invited and declined.

Inclusion would involve change and courage, and risk and love.

There is comfort in remaining the same, even in poverty.

There is comfort in being part of the *out group*.

Sometimes it was because there was no invitation or at least not a sincere one.

Sometimes it was because there was an invitation and a bad experience.

Sometimes there was a deliberate effort not to invite.

It would seem that the efforts of those in the family to reach those outside the family looks more like a waltz of bowlegged introverts dancing in the dark than it does the love of the Body of Christ.

The result is détente.

Détente works for nations that could destroy each other but don't really want to. They don't want to fully reconcile with each other, but they don't want to destroy each other.

Détente is an artificial sweetener. It replaces love.

People say they are in trouble.

We throw some money at the problem.

People say they are hungry.

We throw some food at the problem.

People say they feel judged.

We ignore their problems so as not to offend.

The result is self pity on one end and self satisfaction on the other.

One side feels they are a victim and the other is detached but satisfied they did what they could.

Speaking the truth in love—and surely stepping on a lot of toes that are resting in their respective comfort zone—this is neither family nor love.

Christian fellowship is about inclusion.

Inclusion in worship.

Inclusion in meals.

Inclusion in service.

Inclusion in the fun.

Inclusion in the work.

PoMo Poverty

Inclusion in the challenges.

Inclusion in the rewards.

Inclusion in the commission.

Inclusion in the planning.

Inclusion in the execution.

Inclusion in the truth.

Inclusion in life.


At the end of our Wednesday evening
meals, there is a brief time allocated for
clean up before we begin classes. This
should be an *all hands on deck* exercise for
the able bodied. Some people gravitate
away from the work. It's not that it's hard
work. Wiping off tables, running a
vacuum, taking out trash, and
occasionally washing a few dishes make
up the fifteen minutes allotted.

I have no hesitation about walking up to
someone who has been in the church for
60 years or 60 minutes and handing them

a washcloth or leading them to where we keep the vacuum.  This isn't allocation of a labor force, it is inclusion.

If you come into the family you should expect to be treated as family.

What does that mean?

It means that simultaneously you are the most honored guest and the lowest servant.

It means that you are family.

There is no need for pretense.

There is no timidity.

There are no special privileges.


The family is where you learn love.

The family is where you learn responsibility.

The family is where you learn sharing.

The family is where you learn serving.

## PoMo Poverty

The family is where you learn trust.

The family is where you learn family.

Some who come into the family of faith
have no previous experience in being part
of a family.

You can't teach and you can't learn family
when there is an *in group* and an *out
group.*

Christians have spent too much time
ignoring those in poverty using the
excuse of not wanting to judge.

What we are truly saying is that *you aren't
really family. We would rather throw a
little food or money your way that get
involved in your life*

That dog don't hunt!

We keep trying to build a bridge of handouts from the world of abundance to the world of poverty and it keeps collapsing. It will continue to collapse. Few make it across from poverty to real life.

Newsflash: We were never supposed to build a bridge.

We are to invite—with all the sincerity that is within us—those who are not part of the family into the family. The Family of Faith, the Body of Christ, and the Covenant Community are where poverty is cast aside.

This is where Christians need to *Cowboy Up* and show some backbone.

We should continue to help a little with those in need, but not very much. We should feed the family for a day, not pay the water bill for a month. We should give the person who comes in looking for help a few cans of food not pay their electric bill.

## PoMo Poverty

How can I say this?

How can I say this as pastor of a church
that gives out tons of food?

I can say it because it's time for the
church to stop helping people worship
other gods. We are fully complicit in the
problem.

We have helped people who time and
time again turn their backs on God. We
need to speak the truth in love more than
we need to give out food. Society has
deluded our wisdom.

We have to stop reinforcing decisions that
lead to poverty.

We need to take a lesson from Joshua and
challenge people to choose this day whom
they will serve.

This day!

Choose the gods of money, profanity,
stuff, fear, self-pity, and low character or
choose the one true God.

We—the church—have helped people so much that they no longer have to decide between the gods of this world and the one true God. We help them anyway.

We—the Body of Christ—have subsidized poverty as if it were our mission to do so.

We—those who know the truth and walk in the light—have helped orphan our brothers and sisters.

We—those called out of the world by God—have not been our brother's keeper.

We need to become love—real love, not throw food or money at somebody kind of love—and we must give those in poverty something that they have forgotten was theirs.

A choice.

For those who have always given some food or money, it's tough not to pay that bill.

It's tough not to give out a month's worth of food.

It's tough not to just cough up some cash and be done with the problem once and for all.

Actually, trying to do away with the problem instead of bringing those who are hurting into the family of faith is why the problem is never dealt with.

We—loving Christians—need to challenge those whom we help to become part of the family. We must challenge them to choose whom they will serve.

Giving money and food and clothing time and time again while people serve the gods of self-pity and entitlement is to make an offering to these gods ourselves.

Is this tough love?

No.

This is love.

There is no such thing as tough love.

There are courageous people who will truly love those whom they don't know, but not be content with the latter condition. They will bring those in poverty into the family and treat them as their own flesh and blood.

They will *cowboy up* and really love those who are hurting.

Let's go ahead and discard the metaphor of last century and say we need to **Christian Up** and show some backbone.

We need to **Christian Up** and take on poverty by bringing people into the family.

Tough assignment?

Yes. Only those petitioning God for such a billet and willing to live courageously need apply. This assignment requires speaking undiluted truth while successfully crossing the minefield of judgment. Only love will get us to the other side.

Does this mean that we don't help people monetarily if they don't belong to the church?

Sometimes, that is exactly what it means.

How hard-hearted the church will become!

How distant from the people!

How detached!

That is the spirit of fear talking. And we have been listening to it for too long!

We have the bread of life and living water but we think if we don't put out a buffet for the poor we have nothing to offer.

We have the bread of life.

We have living water.

We have the Truth.

And we need to quit discounting that!


Who among us would turn a blind eye to someone sacrificing their child on an altar to a pagan god?

Are you kidding? We would be all over that. If we didn't intervene ourselves we would call the police, child protective services, or the Marines to stop this atrocity.


I doubt it!


We watch this unfold every day. Parents in poverty are faithful to their gods. Their lives are a living sacrifice to the gods of selfishness, self-pity, entitlement, and fear and we stand by and watch.

PoMo Poverty

Well they are not our kids—who are we to...

Stop them from sacrificing them to a pagan god?

It is time to say:

*Choose this day whom you will serve.*

*The God who liberates or the god who enslaves.*

*The one true God or the god of poverty.*


We must ask this question.

This is our time.

We are God's people.

Let's quit lying to people.  Let's tell them the truth about life.

Let's tell them there is no life without God.

There is no abundance without Christ.

We are asking people to choose life or death.

We are praying and encouraging and inviting people to choose life.

And we are finished subsidizing the road to poverty and death.

We have the words of life.

*Come and be filled.*

*Come and be family.*

*Come and leave poverty and death behind.*


The message we must convey without wavering is that *you were made for life*!


**You were made for life!**

**You were made to live in its fullness!**

*PoMo Poverty*

A Note to the Church...

We sometimes think that fellowship is just getting folks together, usually with food or fun or in the case of most churches, both.

We must never forget though, that fellowship is communion. This is the Body of Christ enjoying each other. That means that we must be vigilant not to become a country club. The least of these must never feel like the least of these within the Body of Christ.

*We must stop measuring poverty in the amount of money or things we have or don't have. A life without God is a one lived in poverty.*

*We who know Christ know the way to abundance. Isn't it time to put an end to poverty and lead many to abundance!*

*Tom Spence*

A Prayer for Koinonia

Lord we pray,

That we seek service over selfishness.

That you open our eyes to the trust you
have placed in us.

That we surrender our God-given talents
and Spiritual Gifts to produce fruit.

That you open our hearts so you may fill
them with love.

That we become your love during this
special time.


That when we are poured out and have no
more, you fill us.

That when we feel exhausted, you refresh
us.

That when we hold on to personal
preferences, you extract them from us.

That when we see no other options, you
ignite the creative spirit in us.

## PoMo Poverty

That when we gravitate to those we know
the best, you lead us to those we know the
least.


That this mission never be a burden,

In our minds,

To our bodies,

For our spirit,

Or in our heart that we have given to you.


That we find your joy as we serve,

Through our sacrifice,

Through our suffering,

Through our humbleness,

And by being love as you are love.

                                        Amen

Tom Spence

*We are family,*

*I got all my sisters with me.*

*We are family,*

*Get up everybody and sing.*

Sister Sledge

Roger Niles

Bernard Edwards

Epilogue

Many find themselves afloat in the sea of poverty.

They are afloat because we not only threw them the lifeline of life in Christ, we just kept on throwing.

Food baskets, angel gifts, helping with a bill, helping with the rent, helping with gas money or money to pay the co-pay on the kid's medicine all seem like acts of mercy individually. Collectively, they are often enough to build a raft and stay afloat on the sea of poverty.

The lifeline of Jesus Christ which is the same lifeline that calls people to live within the family of faith is getting lost in the quasi buoyancy of food, money, and all manner of help. People are making a raft out of a variety of subsidies and find themselves relatively comfortable in poverty with no motivation to reach the safety of abundance.

So what should we do?

*Tom Spence*

Should we stop helping?

If you were drowning in the middle of the ocean and someone threw you a life preserver attached to a life line and you grabbed onto it and they started pulling you towards the ship, would you then want them to start throwing other buoyant materials into the water?

What signal does that give?

The lifeline isn't good enough?

We really don't want you on our ship?

Make a raft and leave us alone?

Go ahead and drown, just take a little longer to do it?

If I am drowning and can't tread water anymore and someone throws me a life line, I want them to pull me in. I am going to start pulling and count on whoever is onboard to be pulling as well.

## PoMo Poverty

I don't want a bunch of clutter in the way.
I don't want anything to distract me from
getting to the safety of the ship.

When I am in dire straits is when I need
to see most clearly.

Poverty or abundance.

Part of the group or an outsider.

Life or death.

When I am in dire straits is when I need
the truth more than anything else.

I may not want to hear it, but I need it.

We need to stop throwing clutter into the
water where we have thrown a lifeline.

We need to be pulling people into the
family of faith instead of throwing
something temporary to them.

This is an *all in* or *all out* deal and we are
called to preach *all in*!  Let's stop
providing the materials for raft building
and bring all aboard the family of faith.

Then Jesus declared, "I am the bread of life. He who comes to me will never go hungry, and he who believes in me will never be thirsty."

John 6:35 NIV

## About the Author

Tom Spence is a retired Marine Corps officer. He has worked as an independent trainer and consultant, an addictions treatment counselor, and as a newspaper manager. He is an ordained minister in the Cumberland Presbyterian Church and is the pastor of the church in Burns Flat, Oklahoma.

He is husband, father, and grandfather and returned to live in his native Oklahoma in 1999.

Tom publishes hundreds of articles online each year as a freelance author, including three blogs and the local paper.

## Other Titles by Tom Spence

<u>Nonfiction</u>

*Throw Away Kids: Are we concerned enough to get involved?*

*God Loves You*

*Heaven and Hell: Why some people can't get off the subject and on with living*

*Technology Acquisition & Front End Analysis for the Small Church*

*ReBaselining America: Setting a foundation of liberty for the next 200 years*

*Christianity for Marines*

*Sea Stories*

<u>Fiction</u>

*Even the Elect*

*First Steps Towards Eternity*

*Tough Day at the Plate*

## Wit and Wisdom Workouts

*The Best of Out of the Box*

## Drama

*9 Encounters of John 9: A Play in 3 Acts*

*Ten Talents: A Play in 3 Acts*

*Clipboard Christmas Skits*

## Life Skills Education

*The Profanity Problem: And what to do about it*

*Acceptance of Authority: Returning to the boundaries of law and ethics*

Tom Spence

www.theburnsflatnews.com

www.thisisoklahoma.blogspot.com

www.thebiasedobserver.com

www.tentalent.blogspot.com

PoMo Poverty

"The King will reply, 'Truly I tell you, whatever you did for one of the least of these brothers and sisters of mine, you did for me.'"

Matthew 25:40 NIV